# Table of Contents

# Disclaimer

# About the Author

A Talent Acquisition leader with extensive background in recruiting & selection interspersed with experience in leading P/L operations and HR generalist role(s) including employee relations, performance management, compensation & benefits and OD.. Pradeep has led & managed recruiting engagements, co-managed as RPO assignments for leading companies, including global brands, such as ST Microelectronic – India, Etisalat – UAE, Telsim – Turkey, Churchill Insurance (now Royal Bank of Scotland, IDC), Schneider Electric India, among others.  He helped these brands scale up from start-up phase to high growth business units in their respective India & Overseas geographies. He has worked in diverse business settings & industry verticals including **Technology, Telecom, Engineering/Infrastructure and Financial Services,** in both corporate & professional services environment.

A keen follower of new and emergent technologies around recruitment & talent management, Pradeep likes to contribute on topical issues in Talent Acquisition including integrating with Talent Management and authors a blog around process, practices & trends that are continuing to impact the recruiting industry. Published online & in print journals by Silicon India, EmeraldInsight.com, LinkedIn.Com, mosaicHUB.com

## What People Have Said About Pradeep Sahay

*We were planning to automate talent acquisition solution. I enjoyed Pradeep's ability to see through end-to-end resource hiring cycle and identify process bottlenecks...* Sunil Malhotra, Vice President, NIIT Technologies

*I liked working with Pradeep due to his professional focus and ability to get results. However, I came to appreciate his leadership style – strategic thinking, empathetic yet firm decision making, strong ethics and rigorous follow through when we worked closely on transforming talent management strategies and practices at four group companies...* Manoj Khare, Partner National Care Organization.

*Pradeep has this unique ability to focus on the overall candidate experience at various touch points in the recruiting process. The same reinforced the employer attractiveness and value proposition enabling a informed decision. A talent acquisition strategist par excellence I would rate him high for his relationship capital...* Prem Swarup, General Manager & Global Practice Head- Business Intelligence, Wipro Technologies, USA

*Working and interacting with Pradeep is a delight - any engagement with him is intellectually stimulating. Pradeep can be credited with nurturing and growing some of the strongest client relationships Datamatics developed in the IT space in Delhi. A slow charming smile hides a sharp intellect that is always looking to bring in innovative changes. He has an unending thirst for knowledge and learning, an eye for detail and very good networking skills-traits that qualify an excellent search professional...* Sumitra Char, Senior Vice President, Datamatics Ltd

*Pradeep is a great business partner, in meeting talent acquisition requirements. Pradeep distinguishes himself by being pro-active, upfront, dependable and a go-getter. He has immense commitment and respect for his partners. His social network and understanding of the talent pool greatly supplement his personal attributes. Despite being an external partner, Pradeep is very supportive of innovative and cost beneficial delivery models which make the relationship more value-adding...* Azfar Hasib, Director HR, Cavium Networks, USA

*Buying Professional Services is rarely a comfortable experience. Unfortunately there seem to be very few professionals who can "hit the ground running" and provide the kind of professional support you need. When we associated with Pradeep as our Professional Service provider, we did not buy into a service, we bought ourselves a relationship - a top drawer Professional Services provider who had the right skills and urgency in recruiting the right person for our organization. The key is - the right kind of attitude & desire to help meet the unique manpower challenges of a rapidly growing organization. As a client he has earned my trust and confidence...* Amit Gupta, Director & Mentor at Fabence.com, ex Managing Director Royal Bank of Scotland, IDC

*Pradeep displayed a professional mind and he could focus on the critical and explain it to the client with empathy. This helps in making informed and effective business decisions...* Emmanuel David, Executive Vice President and CHRO, Volta Ltd (A Tata Group Company)

*Pradeep attended Lean Six Sigma workshop conducted by me in 2012. I appreciate his ability to relate softer intangible human resource challenges with quantitative decision making approaches. He was able to provide valuable inputs during the training on how data driven decision making can be instrumental for HR professionals. It helped other participants to see that HR equally needs efficient processes, not just words. I truly appreciate these inputs and thank him for attending the workshop...* Dr Shantanu Kumar, Director, Benchmark Six Sigma

# Executive Summary

***Did we hire the right person, with the right skills, at the right cost and the right fit?***

Talent Acquisition today, is an activity is fraught with risks and also has the maximum impact on an organization bottom-line. It is more than just posting a requisition and making an offer but a series of sourcing activities, branding efforts, assessment processes, on-boarding activities, and more – all designed to help an organization answer these key questions and find talent relevant to its business context.

Rapid, complex and pervasive changes are occurring in our business landscape that will continue to impact the traditional concepts of work, employer, and employee relationships. As a result companies are getting smarter and innovative about how they acquire talent. They are making their recruitment operations more strategic by connecting external and internal recruitment activities with succession planning and performance management. Balancing immediate needs with long term goals they are improving how they apply people, processes and technology to acquire critical talent. It is this critical talent that go on to create new products and services and find new and innovative ways of dong business. Being more innovative in sourcing and recruiting can give an organization a sustainable competitive advantage by enabling it to find and hire more of the right people who can drive innovation throughout the entire company.

This book is written in the form of an anthology around seminal insights gleaned from the contributions of some *distinguished practitioners from the academe & the business world* and its implications for the discipline of *talent acquisition.* The first four chapters of the eBook examine how principles from the world of quality management and manufacturing can be adapted to create a best-in-class recruiting function and demonstrate the causal connection between 'value-added' recruiting activity and positive business results. The last chapter throws light on how a Design Thinking methodology can truly optimize the function to enhance its strategic impact

Efficiency within talent acquisition coupled with increased customer satisfaction and cost savings are key objectives, now more than ever. Leveraging these learning could help solidify its reputation as a true strategic business partner.

# Chapter I
# Innovative Efficiencies in Recruitment

A Pig and a Chicken are walking down the road.
The Chicken says: "Hey Pig, I was thinking we should open a restaurant!"
Pig replies: "Hm, maybe, what would we call it?"
The Chicken responds: "How about 'ham-n-eggs'?"
The Pig thinks for a moment and says: "No thanks. I'd be committed, but you'd only be involved!"

The fable above echoes the yawning gap Recruiting as a function & Industry must navigate from its commonly perceived role as a tactical support function to one of a genuine *business partner*. The increasingly VUCA environment we find ourselves in & the trends driving today's recruiting marketplace are creating special challenges for organizations in the way they attract & engage with Talent. The shift we are seeing here is one of moving away from the model of *attracting* & *selecting* the best talent to one of *attracting, engaging* & *selecting* the best talent. Another challenge is that talent acquisition has become far more resource intensive than the recruiting function of the past. Resources are needed to develop the employment brand, create referral programs, manage candidate audiences, campus programs and similar such strategic initiatives. Making a strategic impact in the face of pressures to reduce recruitment costs resembles a *Sisyphean task*.

# Recruitment Trends – Circa 2014

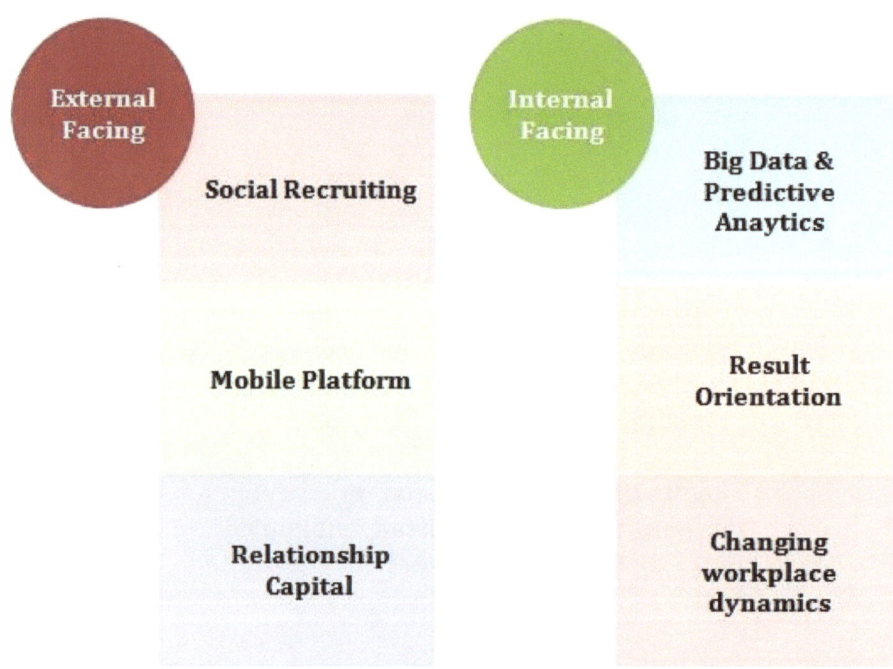

The changing scenario & trends necessitate that the recruiting function create innovative efficiencies to make a visible impact on the organization performance and work as true, *committed* value- adding partners with key stakeholders.

***So how does the recruiting function go about creating innovative efficiencies that drives strong corporate performance?***

The answer probably lies in leveraging some of the innovations we are seeing around us, specifically the advent of *Big Data* and the ramifications it has for recruitments going forward. Imagine functions such as marketing, finance, production proposing solutions to their key constituents unsupported by data points, but the logic of the recruiting function has always been centric around trust  and building relationship capital -the antithesis of analytical, evidence based decision making. While relationships have been and must continue to be the epicentre for the recruiting function it must take its data-savviness to new heights

At its core the real value of Big Data is its ability to give us quantitative insights, throw up patterns from the end user perspective about *where do we currently stand* and *where are we falling behind in our services*. Interpretation of this data can provide us the answer to *what* to do for our end users – hiring managers, business leaders, candidate-in terms of innovation. A word of caution though – As producers and consumers of data analysis it is important that we as recruitment professional are able to differentiate between an unbiased interpretation of data and one that uses data to tell a story.

One could draw a lesson here from **Nate Silver**- the political predictor and the baseball sabermetric man – who didn't just understand data to predict the US Presidential election results with certainty, but understood storytelling & that data must be baked into a broader and better story within a context. Recruiting professionals must regularly evaluate the data and information as it guides and leads the businesses it operates in attracting, engaging & selecting the best talent.

Ability to complement the numerate insights – *the science* with the relationship building – *the art* can help solidify the reputation of the recruiting function as a committed strategic partner. *But this would require the function and the profession to stop being a chicken*

# Chapter II
# What Can Talent Acquisition Learn from Walter Shewhart

Walter Shewhart and the Talent Acquisition

The original notions of Total Quality Management and continuous improvement trace back to a former Bell Telephone employee named **Walter Shewhart**. One of W. Edwards Deming's teachers, he preached the importance of adapting management processes to create profitable situations for both businesses and consumers. A non-obvious contribution of quality management has been the focus on *reducing variation* as a way to improve quality. *When the ancients built their temples they needed squared stones that would fit together. In a high quality car the doors and the frame match with precision.* Customers of talent acquisition would expect such a *talent fit* and as a recent global study by PwC reveals Talent mismatch costs global economy US$ 150 billion

Walter Shewhart pioneered a method of innovation known as the Shewhart cycle, more popularly known in the business world as the **PDCA** or the **PDSA** cycle. The cycle contains four continuous steps: Plan, Do, Check & Act and draws its structure from the notion that constant evaluation of management practices – as well as the willingness of management to adopt and disregard unsupported ideas – are keys to the evolution of a successful enterprise or a function. PDCA is an iterative problem–solving process which starts off small to test potential effects on processes, and gradually leads to larger and more targeted change

The **Exhibit** below presents the key drivers of Recruitment 'performance & business impact' & how the PDCA cycle can be applied to optimize the recruitment function to achieve significant results around cost, efficiency & bottom-line impact.

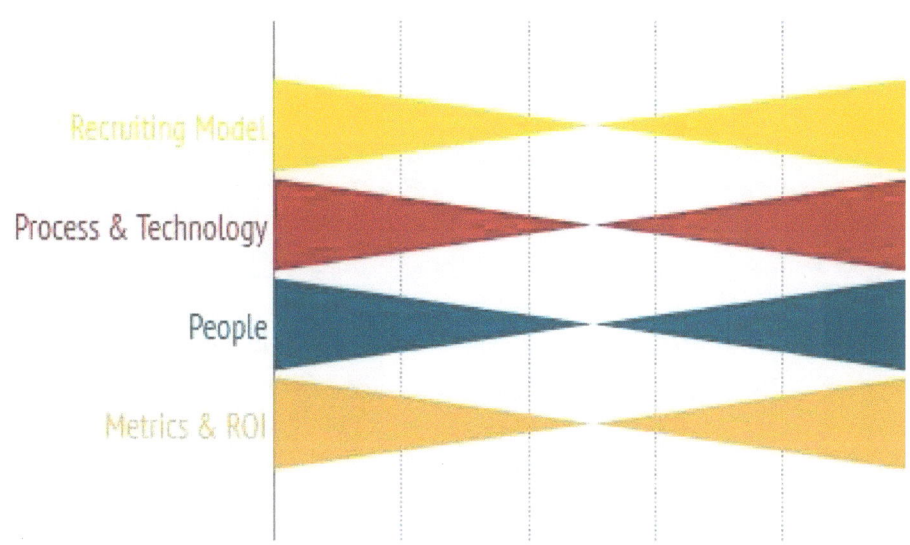

**Plan**: As with any improvement effort, a recruitment deployment plan must begin with clarifying the hiring objectives in consultation with the key stakeholders. An objective assessment of the current state of the Talent Operations – *around the key drivers outlined above* - to understand the gaps that can be addressed, is a key deliverable of this stage

**Do**: The plan must include clear steps, responsibilities and timelines to enable effective execution of the recruitment plan

**Check:** Understanding whether the recruitment plan is progressing on schedule, as well as their effectiveness in enabling the stated objectives to be met are necessary to keep the transformation effort on course

**Act**: Based on the results of the **Check** step, the plan continues as designed or adjustments are made to address the gaps, areas of concern. The precondition for the success is the standardization of the changes to improve the process and their implementation into the new plan

### *Creating & Measuring Value to the Business - The PDCA Way*

Like any improvement effort, talent acquisition optimization is a continuous process, which if executed with a strategic mindset can deliver real value to business in sustainable terms. By assessing the function through the framework of the PDCA cycle, one can establish a strategy that will deliver continuous improvement in talent quality, recruiting process efficiency, recruiter productivity and cost optimization. This continuous improvement will be essential, because in a market where talent, given the right talent practices, is an "appreciating asset" talent acquisition is more than an overhead function, it is a critical capability to drive the success of the business as a whole

# Chapter III
## What Can Talent Acquisition Learn from Taiichi Ohno

The second part of this uncovers learning from the key architect of *Lean Manufacturing* and the opportunity it presents to standardize and streamline the recruitment processes as the pressure to acquire top talent intensifies

*Taiichi Ono and the Lean Way of Recruiting*

Lean operation principles are derived from *lean manufacturing practices* developed as a strategy by the Toyota Motor Company. A management philosophy anchored around the **Toyota Production System** (TPS); its key principles were shaped by **Taiichi Ohno**, a Japanese businessman, widely considered to be the father of TPS. Ohno's principles influenced areas outside of manufacturing and are being leveraged to improve transaction - based service operation - like recruitment. In his groundbreaking book **Going Lean,** author Stephen Ruffa cites standouts such as Walmart and Southwest Airlines as pioneers in adopting Lean to combat a turbulent business environment.The lesson here is that when external market forces are restless, corporations can weather the storm by adhering to the stabilizing forces of lean culture.

## Understanding Lean

The key focus of lean is to identify and eliminate wastes from all processes, a fundamental principle in alignment with the goals of Six Sigma Management System. The **exhibit** below outline the key steps & principles in a Lean Implementation

8 Wastes in Lean - MUDA

**Talent**

Underutilizing people's talents, skills, & knowledge.

**Inventory**

Excess products and materials not being processed.

**Motion**

Unnecessary movements by people (e.g., walking).

**Waiting**

Wasted time waiting for the next step in a process.

**Transportation**

Unnecessary movements of products & materials.

**Defects**

Efforts caused by rework, scrap, and incorrect information.

**Overproduction**

Production that is more than needed or before it is needed.

**Overprocessing**

More work or higher quality than is required by the customer.

Critical to effectively leveraging Lean is the identification of which steps in a process add value to customers and which do not. After classifying process activities into these two categories, the focus is to take steps to improve the former and eliminate the latter

## Lean Concepts & Tools Applied to Talent Acquisition

Applying the lean philosophy to similarly evaluate the Talent Acquisition Process, it is practical to view the components at a granular level. The *exhibit* below illustrates a typical Talent Acquisition process map.

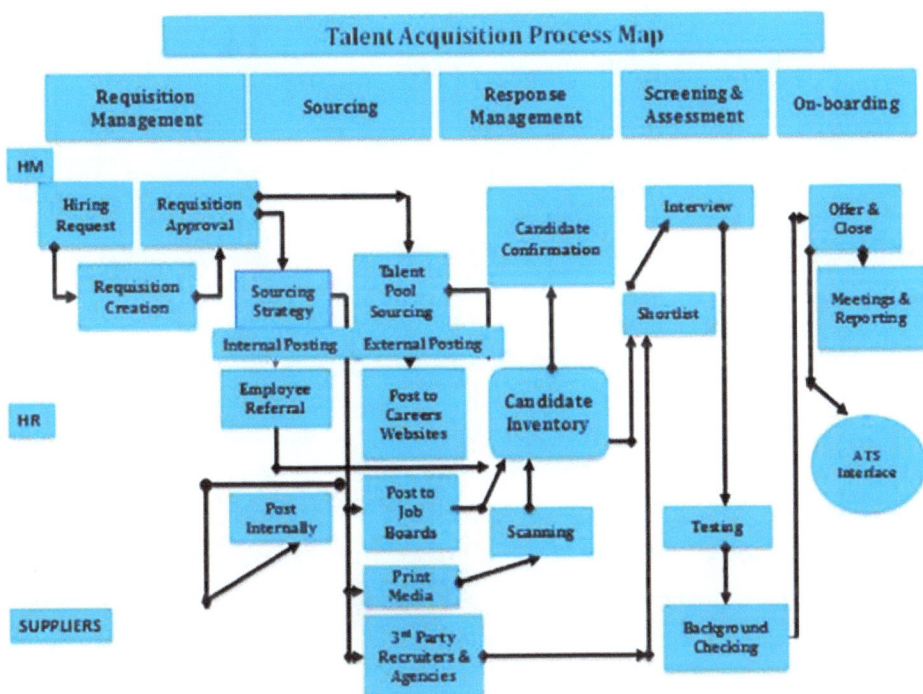

A useful analogy for identifying the areas of improvement is to envisage the recruiting process as a leaky pipe. Process efficiency leaks, or sources of waste in the talent acquisition process can occur in many ways. They could be found in the activities, and practices at each stage of the process and during hand-offs that occur in the cycle of the process. An appreciation of the non-value added activities at each stage of the process could then be evaluated in terms of labour and unnecessary expenses.

| Type of Waste | Recruitment Process Flow |
|---|---|
| Waiting | Evaluations/Approvals, Waiting for feedback,  Indecision, On Hold Candidates, Waiting for Offers |
| Over-Production | Processing prior to the need, WIP Candidate Pipeline |
| Re-Work | Incorrect data, JD's, role appreciation gaps, Improper Stakeholder buy-in |
| Motion | Tracking down paperwork, Time spent on non value add activities |
| Over-Processing | Updating ATS, Duplicating Data Points |
| Inventory | Offers to be processed, Resume Reviews |
| Transportation | Shipping Offer letters, Multiple Interviews, Hiring Process |

The total economic value of the process efficiency leaks or wastes can be optimized to uncover the hidden ROI of the Talent Acquisition Process with tangible business impact.

Tools and concepts such as JIT, Value Stream Mapping, SIPOC, 5S, & Kaizen are integral to the lean manufacturing toolkit. As Lean deals with production system from a pure process point of view, and not a hardware point of view, it has been found that its principles can be adopted to improve the efficiency and speed of all processes in any business context. Just as this management approach is capable of turning out a better product, when *applied to recruitment*, practitioners can expect a more efficient and responsive process to find top talent

In the *section below* we take a quick view on the application of some of the fundamental Lean tenets to a recruitment process

# Voice of the Customer

The Hiring Managers, Candidates (Prospective), Employees are the key customers of the hiring experience. This *'Voice of the Customer'* is the primary variable in understanding the current state of the hiring process and figuring out the key skill & attribute mix in ensuring an optimum QoH-Quality of Hire. Depending on the size of the customer base and the complexity of the initiative,the Voice of the Customer can be a captured form of a supplier, input, process, output, customer **(SIPOC)** diagram or documented using measurement tools such as surveys, interviews, Kano Analysis.

| Suppliers | Input | Process | Output | Customer |
|---|---|---|---|---|
| External Search & Selection partners, Internal Hiring team, Employee Referrals, Internal Talent mobility | Resume, CV, Social media profiles, Performance reviews | Requisition Management, Sourcing, Response Management, Screening & Assessment, Selection & On-boarding | Selected Candidate, Requisition closure, Quality of Hire | Hiring Manager, Business Unit Heads, HR, Employees, Hiring Team, SME's, Corporate Communications, Marketing |

# Value Stream Mapping

A critical lean output, it is a visual representation of the process to be addressed. It attempts to tie together the components of stakeholder value & competitive advantage and consists of process steps, cycle times, people and systems. The purpose of the VSM is to determine where process improvement opportunities exist and demonstrate a clear cause - effect relationship that all stakeholders can align their own action against as illustrated in this **sample case study** - **Value Stream Mapping the Recruitment Process**

**5S** If VSM represents the road-map for the lean journey, then 5S can be considered the gas for the road. The following 5 principles set the foundation on which lean organizations execute their operational plans and help ensure process consistency. When the 5S concept was first introduced, it was aimed at improving production flow on the manufacturing floor; however these principles can be applied with equal success to recruitment, where unnecessary activities impact hiring and service delivery to customers. Each of these tools facilitates waste elimination & minimizes process variation.

### ■ SORT ■ SET IN ORDER ■ SHINE ■ STANDARDIZE ■ SUSTAIN

**KAIZEN** Kaizen is a Japanese word which means to change or modify (Kai) to make things better (Zen) During the implementation stage of 5S, Kaizen assembles small cross-functional teams - stakeholders who can help sustain & administer continuous improvements. It fosters a collaborative environment with a clear focus on eliminating wastes in a process. When a problem is identified a Kanban, is used to visually flag the problem. For instance, if *interview scheduling* often results in conflicts, a kanban is pulled and the kaizen team undertakes a three step approach to resolving the issue, including problem identification, resolution brainstorming, and validation of the problem

**Just in time** A critical lean concept, just-in-time (JIT) is founded on the principle of continuous reduction of all inventory while satisfying changing market demand with shorter lead times and flexible production. A pull based production strategy, the goal of JIT is to deliver just the right amount of supply to meet demand. Applying this concept to talent identification and acquisition, ***Just-In-Time recruiting is a pull-based strategy of providing hiring managers/clients with the right candidates at the right time with the right skills at the right place.*** Instead of proactively building, maintaining a work-in-progress candidate pipeline and creating a Talent Inventory without an actual hiring need, JIT recruiting has a primary focus on tapping into "raw material" candidate inventory (resumes, Social media channels, other sourcing networks) and qualify and deliver a talent pool in direct response to a hiring need.

The [Pugh Decision Matrix](#) is a simple but powerful lean tool for methodically making a choice from several alternatives. This decision making tool applied to a *hiring scenario* is illustrated below

**Sample Candidate Evaluation Summary**
**Pugh Matrix**

Candidate 1- Datum
Candidate 2
Candidate 3
Candidate 4
Candidate 5

| Characteristic/Skill | Importance | Datum | Candidate2 | Candidate3 | Candidate4 | Candidate5 |
|---|---|---|---|---|---|---|
| Strong Work Ethic | 9 | | s | - | s | + |
| Honesty | 9 | | s | - | s | s |
| Integrity | 9 | | s | - | s | s |
| Attitude | 7 | | - | s | s | s |
| Conceptual Ability | 3 | | + | s | - | s |
| Adaptability | 5 | | + | s | + | - |
| Physical Ability | 3 | | - | - | s | s |
| Computer Skills | 1 | | s | - | + | s |
| Writing Skills | 1 | | s | - | s | + |
| Reliability | 7 | | + | - | s | s |
| Pragmatism | 7 | | s | s | s | + |
| Likeable | 5 | | + | - | s | s |
| Ability to Learn | 7 | | s | - | + | + |
| Stress Management | 5 | | s | s | + | s |
| Functional Exp | 1 | | + | s | s | s |
| Sum of Same | | | 8 | 6 | 10 | 10 |
| Sum of + | | | 5 | 0 | 4 | 4 |
| Sum of - | | | 2 | 9 | 1 | 1 |
| Weighted Sum of + | | | 21 | 0 | 18 | 24 |
| Weighted Sum of - | | | 10 | 51 | 3 | 5 |
| Total Weighted Score | | 0 | 11 | -51 | 15 | 19 |

Candidate 1 and 5 are clearly better fitment & hiring cases, Candidate 3 is a clear reject
Candidate 4 can be considered as a back up in the event of a fallout

Embracing some of these Lean best practices in Talent Acquisition, within the larger ambit of Talent Management issues facing organizations, underscores the need for a New Way of thinking about Talent Management. By far the greatest risks in Talent Management are, first, the cost of mismatch in employees and skills and second, the costs if losing the talent development investments through failure to retain employees. By leveraging the fundamentals of Lean manufacturing - identifying value creating activities, eliminating waste, and focusing on continuous improvement - there is an opportunity to lift recruitment to new heights of efficiency and quality with visible impact on the bottom-line.

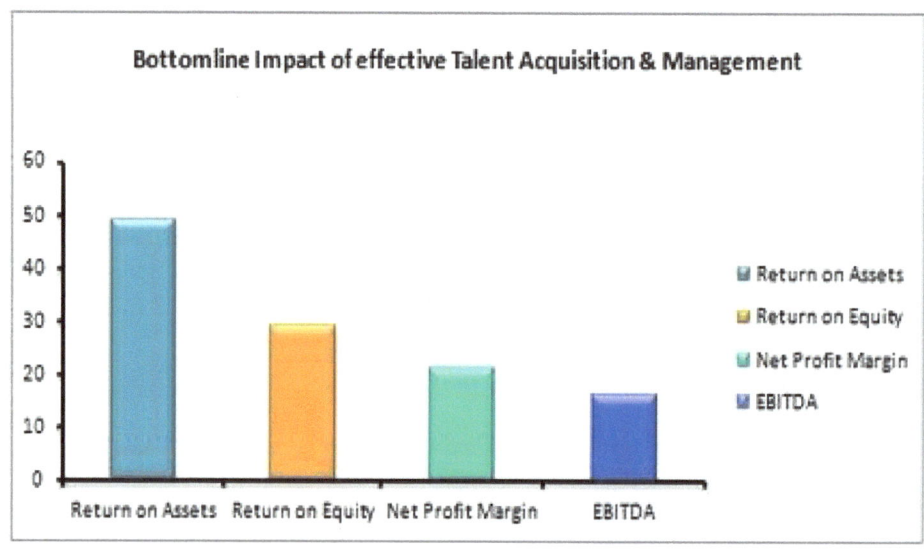

Mucha, R.T. (2004 Winter). The art and science of Talent Management. Organization Development Journal, 22, 96-101

# Chapter IV
# What Can Talent Acquisition Learn from Eli Goldratt

This third and the last post draws insights from one of the foremost management thinkers of our times, who created and developed a framework, which applied to Talent Acquisition can help realize the economic impact of the function with dramatic results

Eli Goldratt's *Theory of Constraints* and the Recruitment *Goal*

The *photograph* above, of a group of clouds shaped as a linked chain being broken through by a hot air balloon, is symbolic of a freedom metaphor of breaking against a *constraint,* and rising above to achieve a *goal*. The Big Idea behind this unassuming portray is a methodology made famous by Dr Eliyahu Goldratt, who conceived the Theory of Constraints and introduced it to a wide audience through his bestselling 1984 novel, The Goal.

The similarities of the manufacturing plant, in this fictional story by Eli Goldratt, and many corporate recruitment departments are striking, and its relevance endures even thirty years after it was written.

**Basics of the Theory of Constraints *applied* to Talent Acquisition**

Shortly after the turn of the century, when *bento boxes* had become Japan's best known contribution to the culinary world, came the widely popular *conveyor belt sushi restaurants*. Also known as **sushi-go-rounds**, the customers, once in, could simply pick little portions of fresh sushi and sashimi of their choice from a moving conveyor belt. The final bill would be calculated based on the number and the type of sushi portions consumed. The idea combined Japanese *minimalism* and their loathing for *wastage*.

The Theory of Constraints (TOC) thinking process similarly draws upon this *minimalist* approach & is built around the core that every process has a single constraint, and that total process *throughput – the rate at which the system makes money through sales,* can only be improved when the constraint is improved. A very important corollary to this is that spending time optimizing non-constraints will not provide significant benefits; only improvements to the constraint will further the goal - achieving more profit.

Thus, TOC seeks to provide precise and sustained focus on improving the current constraint until it no longer limits throughput, at which point the focus moves to the next constraint. The underlying power of TOC flows from its ability to generate a strong focus towards a single goal and to removing the principal impediment (the constraint) to achieving more of that goal.

This concept when applied to recruitment helps us understand the **goal** to be:

**To maximize the number of quality hires/month for the organization ~*Eli Goldratt* calls this 'Throughput'**

and that there is a fixed amount of Time, Money & Resource - *'constraints' that need to be optimized*

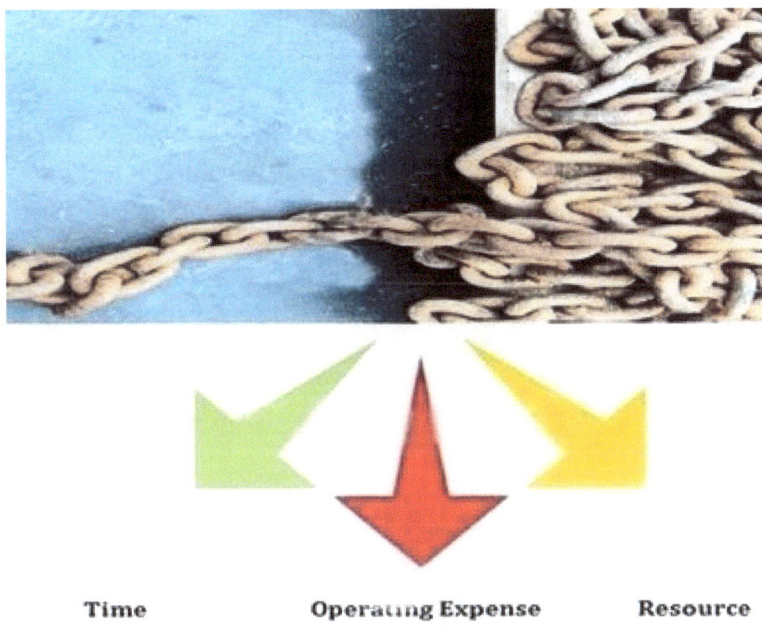

A staffing supply chain when viewed through the lens of *'Throughput and Constraints'* changes the perspective of the function from being transactional driven to relationship driven. It shifts the focus from the *'more is better'* philosophy to how efficient we are with the 'candidate activity we put into the staffing supply chain funnel', and helps organizations evaluate the quality of their hires versus focusing on quantity and cost containment. The *quality of hire* and not the *quantity* should help guide the talent acquisition strategy and tell the story of recruiting effectiveness at both the pre-hire & post-hire level

The Throughput is a great TA metric for these very reasons. Most importantly, it illustrates the efficiency of the entire recruiting process by focusing on *cradle to grave* hiring ratios and help identify low & high performance process zones as exhibited below:

With these data points at display, there is no room for inefficiency, old school recruiting or MacGyver- style selection methods. With *Throughput* everyone sees the value of having a defined role and all stakeholders have a skin in the game

**Focus** is the essence of TOC and using the right metrics, recruiters will be encouraged to focus their behaviors on the causes and not the symptoms of **recruitment success.**

Dr. Eli Goldratt could not have summarized this better when he said:

*"Focusing on everything is synonymous with not focusing on anything. Can we condense all of TOC in one single sentence? I think it is possible to condense it to a single word - focus."*

# Design Thinking Applied to Talent Acquisition

The **Wikipedia** defines design thinking as a style of thinking which combines **empathy** for the context of a problem, **creativity** in the generation of insights and solutions, and the **rationality** to analyze and fit solutions to the context.

While design thinking has become part of popular lexicon in contemporary design and engineering practice, as well as business and management, its principles can be seamlessly applied across multiple disciplines and industries. The premise is that by knowing about the process and the methods that designers use to ideate, and by understanding how designers approach problem solving, individuals and businesses will be better able to connect with and invigorate their ideation processes in order to take **innovation** to a higher level. The hope is to create sustainable competitive advantage in today's volatile global economy which has increasingly become knowledge -based.

## Principles of Service Design Thinking

**Marc Stickdorn** in his seminal work **This is Service Design Thinking** talks about 'How to design and market services to create outstanding customer experiences'. He lays down **5 basic principles**

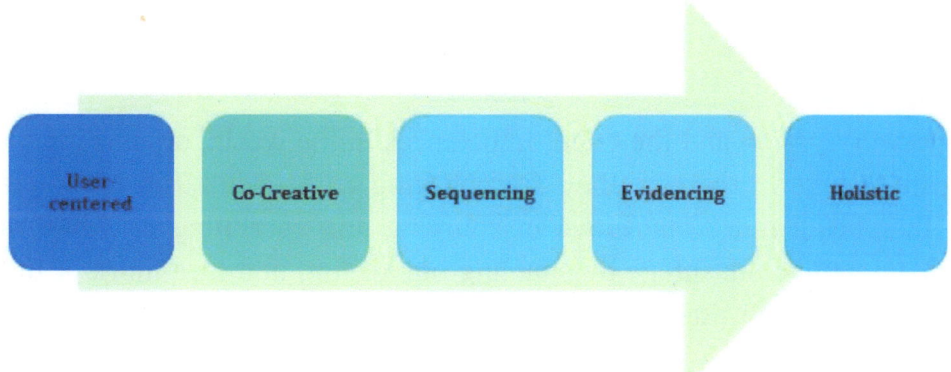

Let us examine here these principles each in turn. <u>**User Centered**</u> means services should be experienced through the eyes of the customer. It is not enough to just look at statistical data about the customers. This pre-supposes a service-oriented mindset. It means listening 'well' to clients, rethinking every communication and interaction no matter how mundane and an attention to detail, an attitude, that is essential if one has to find the self-discipline to handle client servicing with empathy. A professional services provider is as much in the business of managing client's experience with respect to professional services as in the business of executing technical tasks.

I would draw upon here from the *"First Law of Service"*[1]: **Satisfaction equals Perception minus Expectation.** If a client perceives service delivery at a certain level but expected something more or different, then he or she will be dissatisfied. The central challenge in a services setting is in managing not only the substance of what we do for clients but also the clients' expectations and perceptions. **Co-Creative** means working with all stakeholders to explore new needs and processes. And the most important stakeholder is the end-user or the customer. **Sequencing** is how the rhythm of the service impacts the mood of the customer. It is important that the service offering has a consistent flavour to nurture and cultivate a long term relationship capital. **Evidencing** is making the customer or the client aware of the intangibles, the 'behind the scenes' services. This is about the customer 'experience' evidenced in the quality of the service offering and a greater likelihood of customer satisfaction and repeat business if applicable. It is imperative that all services provide some form of artefact to remind the customer a service took place. Lastly **Holistic,** It means keeping the mood and feelings of the customer in mind at all the 'touch-points' in the relationship journey. No detail is small too ignore in the final *customer experience.*

## Can Design Thinking Principles be applied to Optimize the Talent Acquisition discipline?

The following sections of this **concept paper** throws light on the changing contours of the Talent Acquisition function, in the background of dynamic business environment we find ourselves in, and how a **design thinking methodology** can truly optimize the function to enhance its strategic impact.

### The Changing Talent Acquisition Landscape

Given the global recession and the talent imbalances in the world, organizations today are getting innovative in the way they are engaging with talent. There is increasing realization that being more *innovative* in sourcing and recruiting can give them a sustainable competitive advantage by enabling one to find and hire more of the right people who can drive innovation throughout the entire organization. *And therein lies the challenge...*

---

[1] 'Managing the Professional Services Firm', David Maister

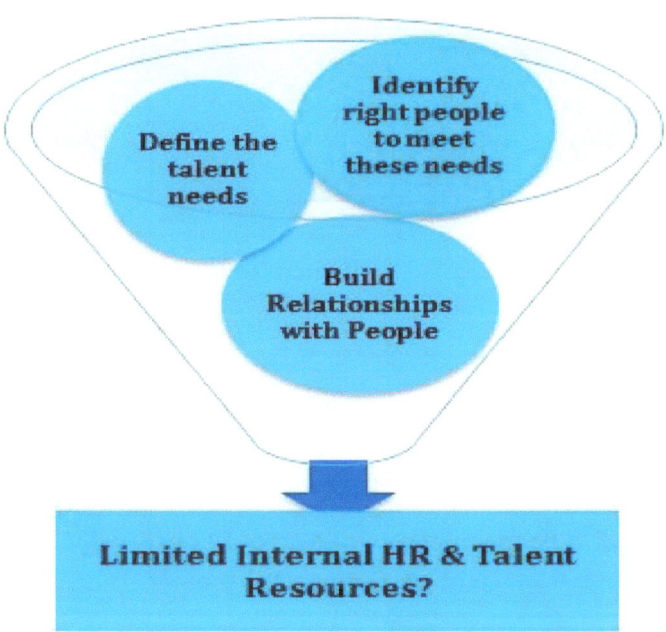

E & Y in its 2008 "Global HR Risk Survey" findings concluded that Talent acquisition & management was seen as the HR risk considered to have the greatest impact on the organization and the most likely to occur. Justifiably so the last few years has seen an incredible shift in how organizations source and hire for talent. The recruiting methodologies and approaches that businesses used in the past are being replaced by new strategies, tools and metrics that are measurably generating high quality candidates. The **exhibit below** captures some of the key elements of the Talent Acquisition framework gaining foothold in the lexicon of Talent decision makers.

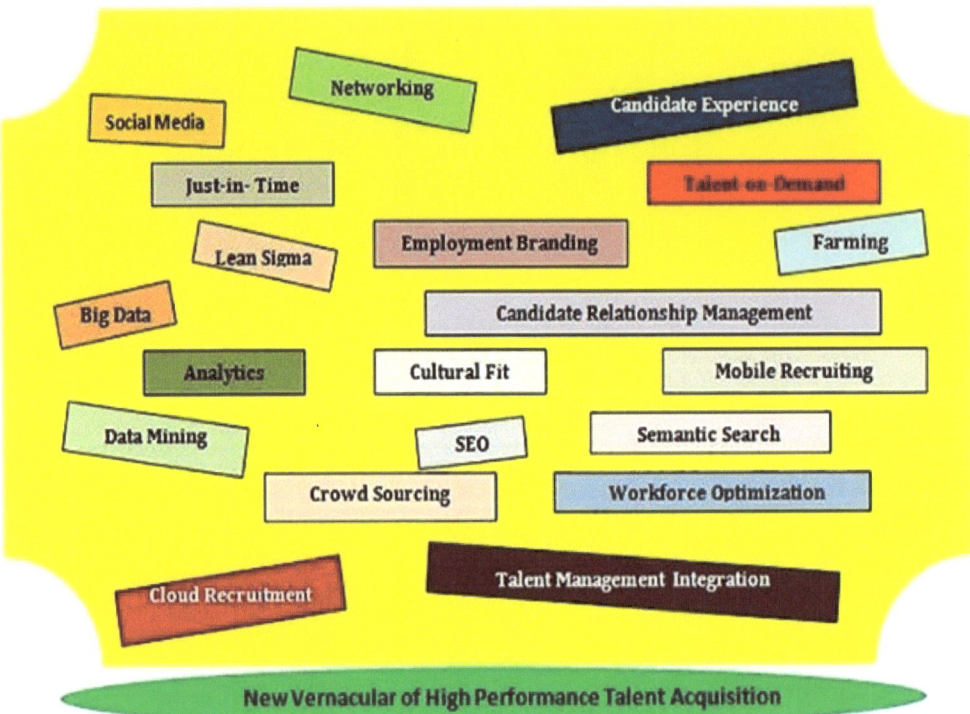

We are today living in an age of global connectivity. Using Ulrich's[2] terms, the **talent war** – *please see exhibit below* - today represents the drive to find, develop, and retain individuals, wherever they are located in the world

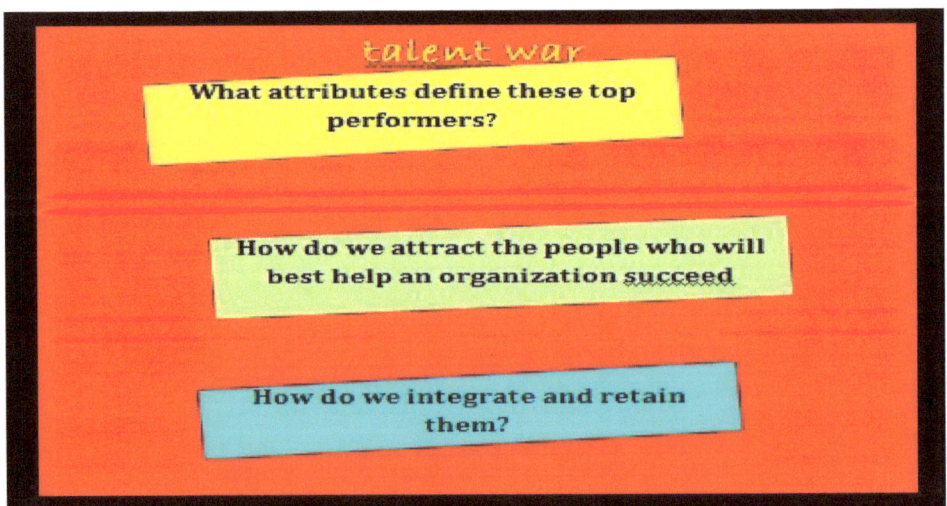

---

[2] Ulrich D.2006. The Talent Trifecta. Workforce Management 32-33 ( September 10)

**Figure[3]** below delineates the talent response dimensions[4] organizations must embrace to attract and effectively engage talent for complex and relationship driven work.

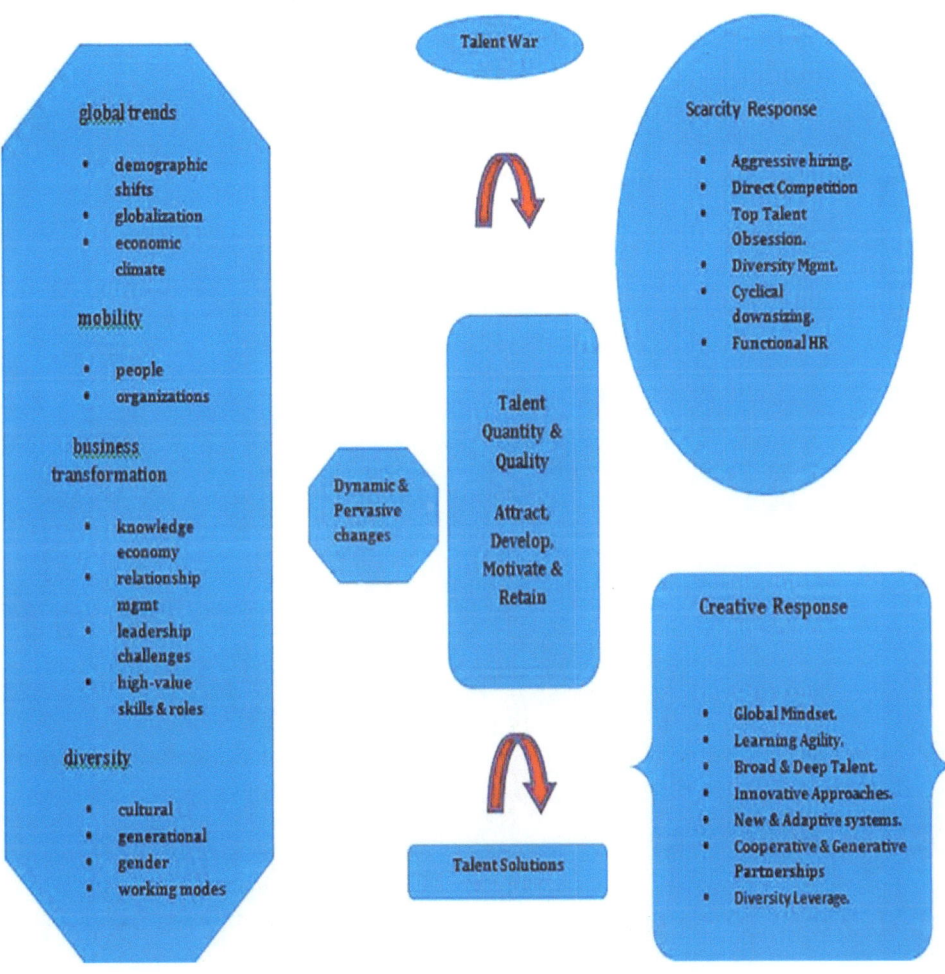

---

[3] The Global War for Talent, Schon Beechler, Ian C. Woodward, Journal of International Management, Fox school of Business, Temple University
[4] Ibid

The Talent response dimensions underscore the pivotal role Talent Acquisition plays in providing a foundation for all Talent Management practices. The key challenge here is to evolve recruitment models which can connect with Talent at large and achieve significant results in terms of cost, efficiency & business impact.
Design Thinking – a human centric interdisciplinary approach towards innovation can help enable such a model.

## Design Thinking Applied to Talent Acquisition

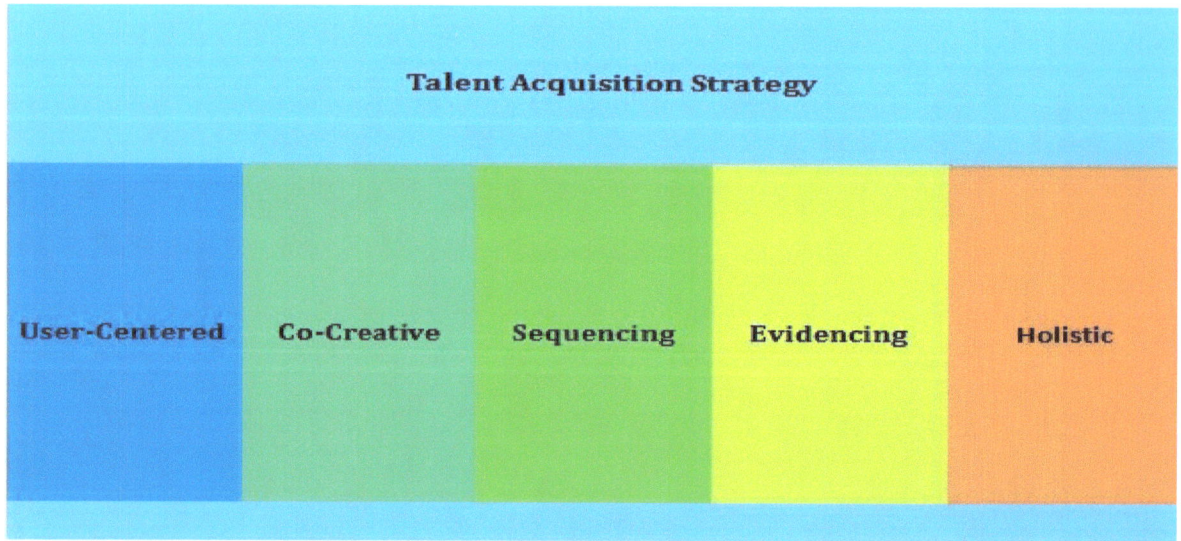

*Let us examine each of the above 5 principles in relation to an organization's Talent Acquisition strategy*

## User - Centered

Customers define **talent's value**[5] and have always paid talent's way. But customers do not necessarily value what talent provides; and they have seldom had direct control over it. The value provided by the "Organization Man" for example, was mostly for internal organization exchange and consumption. This insulation of talent from customer value is changing in the era of customer strategies. The most successful businesses have distinguished themselves by coming to terms with the important but unsettling reality that customers and markets do not care about companies and barely care about the products and services companies sell. In the customer seat, products and services only have visibility and value if they improve customers' lives or contribute to customer success - that is they solve the problems that prompt customers to seek

---

[5] Successful Talent Strategies, David Sears

products and services in the first place. The **Container Store**, a Dallas based speciality retailer of home and office storage solutions, demonstrates **talent value** to customers through its substantial investment in new sales employee education. The retailer delivers 235 hours to new full-time employees during their first year, education that includes point of sale processes, sales skills, product knowledge, and inventory management. By contrast, the norm for the retail industry is approximately seven hours annually. The example demonstrates how the desired customer values were translated into employee performance requirement which is a function of the 'right talent mix' to ensure business success. When we think of it, **employers ultimately do not want employees.** Instead they want the **correct and timely mix of talent** who can either supply products or services customers value immediately or, in the long term, do one or more of the following:

> Increase customer use and value perception of existing products, services

> Develop or find new customers for existing products and services

> Making the connection between what customers value and what talent provides is a recurring new reality

### Key metric to track:

♦ Quality of hire – both at the pre-recruiting & post recruiting stage

The quality of hire should help guide the talent acquisition strategy and tell the story of HR effectiveness at pre and post hire levels. The goal should be to influence the C-suite leadership to buy-in on the quality of hire and invest in the hiring process. It is the most visible manifestation of end user satisfaction

## Co - Creative

Application of this principle to Talent Acquisition (TA) is to underscore the importance of integrating TA and TM (Talent Management) in organizations as the need for – and the scarcity of- specialized talent becomes more critical. Although the two functions have the same overall goals – ensuring the organization has the best talent – the two roles just don't intersect in most organizations[6]. In many organizations, a wall of separation has existed between the TA and TM functions for years. TA operates on its own, separate from HR and TM, while bemoaning the fact that no one gets what they do. At the same time HR business partners and OD professionals often wonder, "What do these recruiters do? How hard can recruiting be?" However the importance of **integrating TA and TM** is something organizations today can ignore at their own peril as hiring manager's demand faster, higher quality talent acquisition and employees demand to know what options exist for them to learn and grow in their career. Technology advances, economic pressures for resource efficiency are all driving the need for a closer integration between the TA & TM roles. The scenario implies defining new roles, processes, trainings and tools. Such changes will require increasing collaboration among all the constituents in the HR value chain within organizations to deliver deeper, more sustainable value for the company and employees.

## Sequencing

The purpose of any Recruitment process is to 'predict' which person will be the most successful in a given role, responsibility area within the ambit of a defined Talent Profile. The more structured the process the better is the qualified success or the quality of the hire. Sequencing essentially is about applying the 'Science' to people decisions which ensures a **consistent, more predictable quality of hire outcome** for the hiring manager, customer. This is about the **'Science of Fit Research'**[7] The process examines the various job roles at work within an organization and diagnose the skills, knowledge, personality traits and experience somebody needs to succeed on these roles. This is accomplished in two ways:

♦ undertake a job analysis and ask workers and managers what they perceive to be characteristics of high performers

♦ Study high-performers and compare them against the average, creating a 'high-performer analysis.'

---

[6] The Intersection of Talent Acquisition & Talent Management, Designs on Talent, LLC.
[7] Bersin Talent Analytics Research

Bersin[8] in its research (using data and analysis provided by Kenexa) looked at a variety of job roles (Sales, Marketing, Leadership) and compared the top 10% of performers in each of the job groups for their skills, knowledge, attributes against the average. The research provided valuable insights on future performance and gave a unique consistent perspective on who to hire by creating the right **Talent Profiles** or **Personas**. These insights form the core of a 'pre-hire assessment'[9] or test and interview script which can help identify top people for a position in any organization.

The combination of assessment tools carefully developed, **sequenced** and executed is critical for the success of any high-performing Talent Acquisition program.

## Evidencing

What gets measured gets improved and by not measuring, the recruiting organization misses an opportunity to learn from its own processes – what it is doing well and how it is adding value to the organization. The final shortlist presentation of a list of prospects to the hiring manager may be the end of the process but making visible the myriad 'behind the scenes' recruiting activities through 'metrics and analytics'- the **Big Data** fuelled hiring- is what can measure the true value creation process in Talent Acquisition and its impact on business results.  Reliable measures linking people to business strategy can impact decision making and investment decisions.

> There is nothing more satisfying than providing a service and demonstrating its value with systematically collected data

---

[8] Ibid
[9] Bersin & Associates: Talent Analytics Research

With the advent of **Big Data**[10], the recruiting function is faced with an unprecedented opportunity to become more data-driven, analytical and strategic in the way it acquires talent. People want to succeed – measurement lets them know when they have. Measurements can be very empowering and the best way to highlight areas that need improvement. The art in measurement is to focus on a core set of indicators that are truly meaningful. Metrics are only valuable if they result in better decisions. Using technology to analyze data is great, but the talent power of data lies in its ability to provide actionable insights (aka – analytics). **In this sense Big Data** can help solidify Talent Acquisition's reputation and raise its value in the eyes of key stakeholders. It can lift Talent Acquisition strategies to a new level of success.

## Holistic

The logic of the Talent Acquisition function is based on building a sustainable relationship capital with the end consumers or client(s) or key stakeholders of the service. For Organizations committed to improving the efficiency of their staffing function this represents a significant point of intelligence. <u>That is successful recruiting ultimately depends on people.</u> Relationships with candidates, hiring managers and HRBP's and the ability to improve the experience of all the constituents at all the touch points in the talent acquisition relationship cycle ultimately drives the success of the staffing function. Companies have come to realize that it can be five to ten times more profitable to build an existing customer relationship to try and create a new one when a customer leaves. It is the same with talent. Despite the shifts in recruiting tactics brought about by e-cruiting[11], the key to the development of a predictable talent flow is having pre-existing and enduring relationships that can be readily converted into work relationships. Recognizing this, some companies are moving to a talent flow approach that mirrors the rationale of their CRM programs.

---

[10] Big Data & Technology, David Bernstein, VP, e Quest
[11] Talent Flow Strategies – Successful Talent Strategies-; David Sears

The logic of talent relationship management (TRM)[12] is that recruiting involves relationships with people who are more like customers than not. Talent relationship management orchestrates with internal and external stakeholders to create sustainable networks of talent supply as into which a business can reach as positions open up. Relationship processes give prospects something of value well in advance of a recruitment pitch. Relationship building however takes time and focus. It operates on different rhythms and thinking than the direct approach. Among the companies adopting this approach is **Electronic Arts Inc.**, a large video game company. It maintains a pipeline of over thirty thousand individual relationships assembled using a web-based ATS, which stores custom talent profiles instead of resumes. The profile data fields capture contact information, information about prospect backgrounds, career aspirations, and geographic preferences. If prospect interests and capabilities match a current opening, the system immediately notifies the hiring manager and encourages the candidate to apply. *This process of developing talent relationships forces managers to develop a more outward-looking view, stay on top of cutting-edge trends, building their company's image and staying in sync with customer expectations. This is but the essence of the **design thinking methodology** – taking insights from people at the various stages, touch points of the process and build from the outside-in rather than from the inside-out.*

---

[12] ibid

# End Notes

As the World Economy continues in its struggle to move ahead from the backyards of recent financial meltdown, dramatic changes fuelled by technology, globalization, demographics & workforce behavioural dynamics are forcing businesses to strategically adapt to new ways to fill talent scarcity gaps. Given the recessionary climate & talent imbalances in the world, organizations today are getting **innovative in the way they are engaging with talent**. There is increasing realization that being more innovative in sourcing and recruiting can give them a sustainable competitive advantage by finding and hiring more of the right people who can drive innovation throughout the organization. While the increasingly VUCA environment we find ourselves in has changed the global business landscape, the forces that drive talent acquisition remain in place. Companies must continue to rely on talent as a core foundation for growth and productivity. At the same time, the need for advanced, specialized talent and leadership will continue to provide challenges for enterprise recruiting efforts.

The structural labour shortage worldwide is changing the way CEO's think about the management of Talent and 'Strategic Talent Acquisition' is being increasingly seen as the fulcrum impacting all Talent Management Practices.

## It's truly an exciting time for organizations with regard to talent

The business and organizational pressures for finding and hiring top talent could not be greater. The real challenge – and indeed the real opportunity- for the profession will lie in learning how to unlock the huge potential presented by emerging tools, techniques and approaches. Recruitment is, and will remain a people centric function but its future promise to provide competitive advantage would be more at the intersection of people with business, process, technology and organization strategy. Leading companies have been seizing the opportunity to move their capabilities forward and creating true competitive advantage in talent sourcing and acquisition. Their benchmark recruiting best practices and strategies are helping elevate recruitment from a transactional, short-term focused activity to a strategic, integrated, long –term approach that optimizes their investments in people.

# References & Photo Credits

■ Walter A Shewhart, 1924, and the Hawthorne Factory: M Best & D Neuhauser

■ Goldratt, M. Eliyahu and Cox, Jeff, The Goal, North River Press Inc., 1992.M

■ Tomas Florian/;Bevan Von Weichardt – *shutterstock* – Chapter II

■GoLeanSixSigma.com; *6kor3dos*; *tomertu*; *gst*; *Yabresse*/shutterstock www.sorach.com/pughmatrix.php - Chapter III

■ Sigrid Klop; Karen Roach/*shutterstock* - Chapter IV

■ www.resourcesystemsconsulting.com – Walter Shewhart Image

■http://www.tomhcanderson.com/wpcontent/uploads/2010/05/eligoldrattchinaindia tomhcandersonanalyticsglobalization.jpg - Eli Goldratt Image

■http://t1.gstatic.com/images?q=tbn:ANd9GcQ2yK8-lowasx2N0Wn-E99lEKvOtxOZykkm6s0pnIL4VaGb1W78 – Taiichi Ohno Image